First Facts®

Earn It, Save It, Spend It!

Spend Money

by Mary Reina

PEBBLE
a capstone imprint

First Facts are published by Pebble
1710 Roe Crest Drive, North Mankato, Minnesota 56003
www.mycapstone.com

Library of Congress Cataloging-in-Publication Data
Names: Reina, Mary, author.
Title: Spend money / by Mary Reina.
Description: North Mankato, Minnesota : Pebble, [2020] | Series: First facts.
   Earn it, save it, spend it! | Includes index.
Identifiers: LCCN 2018060536| ISBN 9781977108333 (hardcover) | ISBN
   9781977110046 (pbk.) | ISBN 9781977108531 (ebook pdf)
Subjects: LCSH: Money—Juvenile literature. | Consumption
   (Economics)—Juvenile literature.
Classification: LCC HG221.5 .R454 2020 | DDC 332.024—dc23
LC record available at https://lccn.loc.gov/2018060536

Editorial Credits
Karen Aleo, editor; Sarah Bennett, designer; Tracy Cummins, media researcher;
Kathy McColley, production specialist

Photo Credits
Capstone Studio: Karon Dubke, Design Element, Back Cover; iStockphoto: Steve
Debenport, 9, vgajic, 21; Shutterstock: antoniodiaz, 5, grey_and, 7 Bottom, John
Brueske, 11, Kim Reinick, 19, LifetimeStock, 7 Top, Nestor Rizhniak, 15, Nik
Merkulov, Design Element, Rawpixel.com, 17, Stokkete, 13, Thomas J. Sebourn,
Cover

Printed and bound in China.
1671

Table of Contents

CHAPTER 1

Spending Choices

Think about the last time you spent money. Maybe you bought a new toy or a book. When people spend money, they trade it for things they need and want. Needs are food, clothes, and school supplies. Wants are things that are nice to have. Toys, candy, and crafts are wants.

When spending money, needs should come first. Pretend you have $2.00. You need a notebook for school. You want a candy bar that costs $2.00. Your money will be gone if you buy the candy bar. And you still need the notebook.

Needs and wants are either **goods** or **services**. Goods are things people buy or sell. A service is work done for other people like cutting someone's hair. Buying goods or services makes you a **consumer**. When you buy anything, such as a candy bar, you are a consumer.

What Are Services?

You do a service when you help at home. Setting the table is a service. People are often paid for a service. A nurse is paid for helping sick people. The nurse is providing a service.

goods—things that can be bought or sold

services—work that helps other people

consumer—someone who buys or uses goods and services

CHAPTER 2

Even More Choices

People can choose to spend money in different ways. Some people use **currency**. This is the form of money used in a country. The United States uses paper bills and metal coins. Many other countries use paper bills and coins too.

FACT

Currency is anything people **value** as money. In the past, people used shells, cows, and cocoa beans as currency.

currency—the type of money a country uses

value—to believe something has worth

You might use a **credit card** when you are 18 years old. It is a small plastic card used in place of money. A credit card lets people **borrow** money.

FACT

A person pays **interest** if only part of a credit card bill is paid. Interest is the cost of borrowing money. The money paid back is more than the items cost.

credit card—a small plastic card used in place of currency

borrow—to use something that belongs to someone else with permission

interest—the cost of borrowing money

A credit card company pays for the items. Then the company sends a bill each month for the amount owed.

Someday you might want to buy something that costs more money than you have. You might want to buy a car. You could ask for a **loan**. Bank workers decide if you can borrow the money. Banks give out loans to people. The people who get the loans pay the money back in smaller amounts over time.

loan—money that is borrowed with a plan to pay it back

It is not as easy as it seems to use credit cards and loans. A buyer could end up owing too much money that cannot be paid back. Then the buyer can have trouble paying the bills.

FACT

People often have to be at least 18 years old to get a bank loan. They must be able to earn enough money to pay back the loan.

CHAPTER 3

Try It!

You can save money and get the things you need. Food shopping can show you ways to spend less and keep more money.

Start by collecting coupons. A coupon has an amount to save on an item. It is given to the cashier when paying for the item. That amount comes off the bill.

Many stores also have sales. Sale items cost less. Stores have signs that advertise, or show, the new price. Find coupons and sales, and then go grocery shopping with an adult. How much did you save?

Brands

When you buy a product, such as cereal, you have choices. You can buy a brand name or the store brand. Store brand cereal might be cheaper than brand name cereal. Yet both items could have the same ingredients. Always check the ingredients and prices before making a decision.

You will always have money choices. Good habits will help you spend less.

Glossary

borrow (BAHR-oh)—to use something that belongs to someone else with permission

consumer (kuhn-SOO-mur)—someone who buys or uses goods and services

credit card (KRE-duht KARD)—a small plastic card used in place of currency

currency (KUR-uhn-see)—the type of money a country uses

goods (GUDZ)—things that can be bought or sold

interest (IN-trist)—the cost of borrowing money

loan (LOHN)—money that is borrowed with a plan to pay it back

service (SUR-viss)—work that helps others, such as providing medical care, fixing cars, or cutting hair

value (VAL-yoo)—to believe something has worth

Read More

Higgins, Nadia. *Using Money*. Money Smarts. Minneapolis: Jump!, 2018.

Reina, Mary. *Make Money Choices*. Money and You. North Mankato, MN: Capstone, 2015.

Waxman, Laura Hamilton. *Let's Explore Spending Money*. A First Look at Money. Minneapolis: Lerner Publications, 2018.

Internet Sites

The United States Mint—H.I.P. Pocket Change Kids Site: Games
https://www.usmint.gov/learn/kids/games

The United States Mint—It Makes Perfect Cents polls
https://www.themint.org/polls/

Critical Thinking Questions

1. Pretend you have $2.00. You need a notebook that costs $1.00. You want a candy bar that costs $1.00. What will happen if you buy both?

2. How do you use a coupon?

3. What is a sale?

Index